I0191650

God, Is She Ready Yet?

A Pastor's
Heart for the
Bride of Christ

Camelot Shuff

To My Amazing God who welcomed me, forgave me, and gave me the life that I never dreamed I could have. You truly are all that I need and I am satisfied in Your Presence.

Through my family and friends, Father, You continue to show Yourself faithful to me.

Through...

My husband, Sam, Strength and Perseverance

My daughter, Emily, True Compassion

My mom, Janice, Hope-filled Perspective

My daddy, James, a Well-lived Life of Faith

(I'll be along shortly to gaze at His face with you, daddy.)

My step-mom, Peggy, Worshipful Dependence

My brother, Clint, Heartfelt Loyalty

The rest of my family, Open Doors and Open Hearts

PK, PV, PM and the HFCN Church Family, Holiness unto the Lord

Special Thanks to Abigail Green, the author of the article, "Here Comes the Bridesmaids!"

God, Is She Ready Yet?
Published by Fleur De Lion

Fleur De Lion is a name I made up to have a cool picture on the back of this book. The picture is of a fleur de lis over a picture of the Lion of the Tribe of Judah and if you look closely you can also see the Lamb. The picture is blurry and unclear except within the outline of the fleur de lis. For me this depicts the vastness of God, yet captures the reality of His choice to reveal Himself through Jesus Christ and the Church, the body of Christ.

Let us represent Him well!

God, Is She Ready Yet?
Copyright © 2014 by
Camelot Shuff

ISBN 978-0-615-64751-7

All Rights Reserved. This book may not be reproduced or distributed in any printed or electronic form without the prior express written permission of the author. Please do not participate in or encourage piracy of copyrighted material in violation of the author's rights.

Table of Contents

God, Is She Ready Yet?

Prologue

Well done good and faithful servant.

Do your ears long for these words to be spoken from the lips of Jesus as He welcomes you into His Kingdom? Mine do. I have served the Lord by way of serving His Church since I was 20 years old after a very rebellious youth. Since then I have been taken in by the family of God, taught the basics of Christianity, and mentored while serving within and alongside the church. While I have been a Christian for almost 20 years, I have been Baptist, Pentecostal and now Nazarene by way of denomination. Every church I have been too has given me more insight into the Big "C" Church of Jesus Christ, The Body of Christ universal. I believe His Kingdom will come on earth through His people, the Body of Christ.

In the transition from one place of ministry to another, my type A personality had me working harder and harder to "accomplish His will". Along the way, my mentors and leaders have helped me to ask the questions that lead me into seeking the Lord and serving Him with the gifts that He has given to me. My heart longs to serve the Lord who truly has forgiven me much. Most days I am overwhelmed with gratitude as I think about where God has led me and allowed me to serve. As my thoughts linger a little on the mount of gratitude, my heart wants to serve all the more, so I work harder. Maybe you understand or experience this yourself. I can make it holy and say that I am serving God will all my heart, mind, and soul, but I want you to know where I was. I surrendered my life to Christ, but it seemed I was running myself into the ground "for Him". I am sure that is not what He intended.

A couple of years ago, I was at "Come to the Fire", a conference for women. Right at the beginning a woman stepped up to the platform and asked if we would bow our heads for two minutes of silence and ask the Lord if He had anything He wanted to say to us. I did. Not really expecting Him to say anything specific. But, He did.

I heard Him say, not audibly but louder than that, "You are in my plan." Of course, in my mind I responded, thank you, Jesus, yes I know I am in your plan. He said again, "You are in my plan." I said, I am excited, Lord. Hallelujah! (I am dense most of the time, even God has to speak a few times for me to get it. He said a third time, "You are not just a part of my plan, you are in my plan." I was silent.

In my life I have gone through the divorce of my biological parents, then my mom remarried, and I grew to love another father and he left when I was 19. I never felt like I was all in the family. Everyone in my family loves me and they did everything in their power to always make me feel a part, but just because of the nature of broken families, if you are with one family it means you are apart from another. All of the big days of my life and holidays had to be celebrated twice or I had to choose. While two Christmases are wonderful! You understand at this point the depth of the healing that my Father was giving to me. I am in.

After a few weeks, I realized though that the drive to serve "gung-ho" was gone. There was a rest I had not known at work within

8

me. For this rest, I am truly grateful. It is a rest of Presence, not necessarily physical rest only. However my mind started to wonder, as a pastor, I was not making the time, buzzing around like I was before. I could not muster it up, nothing. That is when God started painting a picture for me that is found in the following pages. He is teaching me how to lead, how to serve and lead at the same time. As a pastor, I am to serve the Lord in a specific way, not by just doing. But rather teaching others and stepping aside so that they can experience the joy of loving and serving God with their whole mind, soul, and strength.

While this book mainly helps one grapple with a call into ministry or even with how you are doing in ministry, the big picture is that of the characters in a wedding, or should I say "The Wedding". The Wedding Supper of the Lamb will be the first of many family reunions of the Church. But before we look ahead, let's catch up a little bit...

Chapter One

God Has a Plan

The most beautiful adjective describing God is Holy, Holy, Holy. Throughout history, God has been revealed and characterized by many different names, but the one adjective that is used three times over for Him is HOLY. Within this description there are many explanations to try to describe what Holy means. Holy. Set Apart. Altogether Other. Whole. Complete. Worthy. Revered. Yet this God who is all powerful, altogether good, and all-knowing considers us His creation. That He even considers us is amazing. David wrote in Psalm 8, "What is man that you are mindful of him? The son of man that you care for him?" But Holy God has not only considered us, but chooses to reveal Himself through us. Our Holy God has a plan. His plan includes us. We who have been given free will are entrusted with the work of God that he has prepared in advance for us to accomplish. His plan is in the work of our hands. His plan depends on us to a degree.

Let's begin with a cliff notes journey of God's plan. From the very beginning, God had a purpose and plan when He created the world and everything in it, including human beings. He not only had a purpose for us, but since He place all created things under our care, this purpose or plan is dependent upon us fulfilling His will. Throughout the Old Testament, we are told amazing stories of men and women who have obeyed the will of God. We also have stories of failure, unfaithfulness and disbelief.

Adam and Eve walked with God until the plan God set before them was sideswiped by sin. God, in full pursuit, spoke to Noah, who obeyed. Instead of wiping out all of His creation, Noah and his family became the restoration of the "crown of God's creation" to life. Another interesting vessel of God was Abraham. God spoke to Abram, "Go to a land that I will show you." Abraham in faith believed God; this faith restored not just life to the human race, but relationship with God. The part that I find interesting is that the Spirit of God was looking for someone to have faith and believe. He was looking for someone who would do the will of God. Abram was not the first person God approached. The beginning of the story begins in Genesis 11:31, "Terah took his son Abram, his grandson Lot (son of Haran), and his daughter-in-law, Sarai, wife of his son Abram. They set out together from Ur of the Chaldeans to go to Canaan. When they came as far as Haran, they stayed there." When I read the last three words in this passage, my mind says, "They stopped short." This is one of the saddest parts of the Old Testament. Terah was headed to a place that his descendants would be promised. I believe that God's plan was revealed to Terah first, and while he began the journey, he did not follow through. We could be talking about the God of Terah, Abraham, and Isaac instead of the God of Abraham, Isaac and Jacob. God's plan continues. He is long suffering and kind, constantly on mission to reconcile us to Himself. Abraham continued to obey God with His son, Isaac. God's desire is to give us life, be in relationship with us, and to bless us. The journey was underway as Abraham trusted God, even with the life of his son.

Saul, whom David calls "anointed of God" was to lead God's people, but in disobedience, he was replaced by the man after God's own heart. David became the king that the people wanted and while his heart was after God, his descendants continued to stray from the heart of God until…

Jesus, a descendent of David, fully God and fully man came to do the will of the Father. He came and lived in perfect obedience, praying "Thy Kingdom come, Thy will be done, on earth as it is in heaven. Jesus came to fulfill the Law and the Prophets. Now that God has redeemed us and made a way for personal relationship and oneness with Him, Matthew 28:19-20 reveals to us, it is the will of God that all men be saved and this will be carried out by His people, the Church. While there are many ways in which the will of God is revealed through us, the apostle John shares the plan and command of Jesus, "Everyone will know that you are my disciples because of your love for each other." Looking back over history, surely the God who pursues us and is zealous for the reconciliation of His creation to Himself continues even today. His plan and purpose is the dwelling of God would be with man. He shall be our God and we shall be His people. The future of the Church is bright. Our God, The Alpha and Omega has promised us a forever in His Presence.

My first introduction to what the Word of God says about God's plan for His Church was before I ever knew Christ. He was pursuing me, but I did not even know it. I did not grow up religious; I grew up rebellious. During my teenage years, I was a heavy drinker and heavier drug addict. After dropping out of college, I turned my life to pursue partying as a career. For a year, I lived like I always wanted to with no rules or expectations. I was having a great time, eating, drinking and being merry, with no thought of the future. One evening, I had some friends over and while we were losing our good sense, a friend took out his bible. He said he was a Seventh Day Adventist and that he could prove the whole world was going to church on the wrong day of the week. In the spirit of rebellion, I argued with him throughout the night using what little I knew about the bible. The night ended and everyone went home. The next morning I woke with a more than usual sluggishness. So much so that I sat there looking around the den. Yep, there sat the bible. I thought, "I know that book has an 'In the beginning', I wonder, does it have an end?" For the next two hours I was engrossed in reading and rereading the book of Revelation. I understood that day in a way that I do not even try to understand now. I called my boyfriend at the time and told him to come home right away because Jesus was coming back. I know that seems silly, but to be honest, I was more sober minded that day that I had been in years. While it took a few weeks from that moment for us to understand and enter into relationship with Jesus, it was that day that I realized God had a plan for me and it was good.

The Bridegroom is coming for His Bride. No one knows the day or the hour, except God the Father, but the future is planned by The Alpha and Omega Himself. I was talking to a couple of pastor friends of mine about the Song of Songs. One of my friends said he had been studying history and as the book of Romans is to us in this generation, so was the Song of Songs to the early disciples, because it represented the love relationship between our Bridegroom, Jesus and His Bride, The Church. My other friend said as she was finishing her masters in church history, she came across the same idea except that this book of love was treasured by the mature believers. Please take that into consideration as we move into the other parts of this book. I believe that God is calling His Church to be yielded to His plan. I believe that He is constantly revealing His plan yes to us as individuals, but I believe more importantly He is revealing to us and through us corporately. This is not a schedule or book about when, but rather a book about reconciliation and response to what the heart of God is revealing to His people.

The timing of Jesus' return is important to me. Not to know the time, but to understand from a somewhat different perspective. It is true that no one knows the day or the hour except, God the Father. Not God the Son or God the Holy Spirit. I was more confused by the fact that One Person of the Trinity would know something that the other Two would not. At least it did until I became the parent of a teenager. My daughter, Emily, is a wonderful girl, who is respectful and honest. However during some of her "learning experiences" she has had consequences that help her to remember not to lie and not to disobey. Once I took her privileges away for a period of time and of course her first question to me was "When can I?" I said that I would let her know when it was time. Did that mean that I knew exactly what time she would be reinstated to full privileges…no. That meant that depending on her attitude, motive, respect level, and response, her actions would let me know she was "ready".

Let me explain "ready" from a different vantage point. As a woman, more of my time is taken up with "getting ready" than most men. Women get ready daily and depending on what or where she is going, she is able to skip steps on different days, like washing her hair or doing her nails. However when she has to get ready for a big event, such as Easter Sunday, prom, and especially her wedding, everything changes. Usually getting ready starts days in advance, which is actually the pre getting ready stage. This would include things such as getting your hair cut, maybe colored, manicure, pedicure, last minute fittings, practice hair styles, facial, etc. Then on the big day, she must get an early start. There is actually a tipping point in which she can change her answer to, "Are you ready to go?" from "not yet" to "almost". For men, they simply hear, "No." But in the process of getting ready, "not yet" means that if we had to go right now, I would have to cancel, there is no way that I can begin the walk to the car in this state of being. "Almost" means that if I had to go, I could grab my lipstick, hairbrush, and jewelry on my way out the door and put the finishing touches on in transit. At this point you think I have gone to writing another book, but the point is that the tipping point for the woman to get herself ready exists when for the most part is she is ready to go... understanding that she could put on finishing touches for another hour or two if given the time. As the Church, the Bride of Christ, I believe we have to ask ourselves are we ready yet? Yes individually, we have to ask the question, but as leaders we also have a responsibility to ask corporately, is the Church ready yet?

There are many signs of the times. While I know that they are significant in history and certainly play a part in the plan of God. Israel became a nation again and other external circumstances, yet I believe the one sign the Father is waiting on is in us. I hear His heart, "My Son, the Bridegroom is ready, He has prepared a place for us, He is sitting at my right hand interceding for you, He is praying the same thing He prayed for you right before He died for you, that they may be one as we are one—I in them and you in me—so that they may be brought to complete unity. (John 17:22-23)" I believe that the Father looks from His throne, He keeps checking, He keeps asking, Is She Ready Yet?

Many scriptures speak to the kind of Bride, Church, that Jesus is returning for. In Hebrews 9:28, Paul writes, "Likewise, Christ was sacrificed once to take away the sins of humanity, and after that He will appear a second time. This time he will not deal with sin, but he will save those who eagerly wait for Him." The culmination of the Church Age is the Wedding Supper of the Lamb. The bride will be united with her Groom in answer to His prayer in John 17. The following chapters explore the wedding party: the Groom, the bride, the bridesmaids, and the Father. Specifically if you are a leader in the church or are grappling with a call to ministry, this book explores this call and God's purpose. Even if you do not consider yourself a leader, you are an influencer as a living testimony to Christ and the heart of the call remains the same, that we be ready.

Chapter Two

The Groom

Jesus Christ, our Bridegroom is the chief cornerstone of all of "HIS"tory. He is the Way, the Truth, and the Life. I could go on forever to tell you of the One called Wonderful who the Gospel writers said there was not enough room in the world to hold the books that could be written about all that He did.(John 21:25) The Groom does not change, but our perspective of Him does over our faith journey. The more He reveals about Himself, the more we love Him. He is holy, holy, holy, worthy of all praise. He is love. Rather than attempt to describe the indescribable, let's look instead at the intimacy of our relationship with Jesus. How do we increase our intimacy and knowledge of our Lord Jesus?

Most people struggle believing God loves them. However, after that truth sinks in on the inside even a little bit, we know, "we love because He first loved us." (1 John 4:19) I am reminded of the score of a young girl plucking the petals off of a flower. He loves me, he loves me not, he loves me, he loves me not... You can be as ecstatic as she would be as she pulls the last petal and says, "HE LOVES ME!" because Jesus Christ loves you and me. I never get tired of saying that out loud. Try it... Jesus Loves ME!

Knowing the Groom loves the bride eclipses her mind and gives her the passion in her preparation for Him and by Him. We are in preparation, being transformed into the image of Christ, not growing weary, but always persevering toward the goal.

With the Bride of Christ, the end goal is the same goal that a woman has in her mind the entire time she is getting ready… to be beautiful, not only to her husband, but also to everyone who will be present for the event that will change her life. With regard to even the wedding party, the goal is for the bride to stand out as the most beautiful woman there. We begin then with the question: How are we made beautiful in the eyes of the One called Wonderful? The One who looks on us with love, how do we please Him?

The attributes of a beautiful Church are the righteous deeds of the saints; that's true, but the eye of the Beholder is Jesus Christ. Remember Jesus is the one who is called the Word of God and Hebrews 4:12 lets us know the extent of His eyes, "For the Word of God is alive and active. Sharper than any double-edged sword, it penetrates even to dividing soul and spirit, joints and marrow; it judges the thoughts and attitudes of the heart." Our beauty must be much deeper than the actions and deeds that are seen. Our innermost being, or our heart, must be beautiful as we in hope await our Bridegroom. 1 Peter 1 gives us insight on how:

> Therefore, with minds that are alert and fully sober, set your hope on the grace to be brought to you when Jesus Christ is revealed at his coming. As obedient children, do not conform to the evil desires you had when you lived in ignorance. But just as He who called you is holy, so be holy in all you do; for it is written: "Be holy, because I am holy."

Be holy; I used to really stumble at this verse because I thought that holy meant perfect, but I was only half right. God is perfect but at

His very essence He is called Holy, Holy, Holy. There is only one other word that is used as an equalizing definition of God. 1 John 4:8 says God is Love. He is the very definition of Love and the very definition of Holy. In 1 Corinthians 12:31 the most excellent or beautiful way is given to us; the Love Chapter follows in great description. John Wesley combined these words or thoughts together calling this Perfect Love or Christian Perfection. Perfect meaning that there is nothing else needed, because it is complete. We say that God is perfect because He is the Holy Other, the One who does not need anything in order to exist and be complete. He is altogether self-sustaining. We can never be that. We can never be perfect in that sense; however, the Bible says we are complete in Christ. We must breathe and eat and have relationships with people to exist as humans. We are dependent, but in Christ because He supplies all of our needs, He completes us.

There is one distinction here that sets us free once we yield or surrender to it. We can be complete in Christ because we are forgiven, but that is just freedom from the penalty of sin. The blood of Christ has also provided us freedom from the power of sin, which is the link that our carnal nature has with temptation. Our heart and motive can be cleansed. As we let go and let God in our life, the divine nature sources us instead of the carnal nature. It is better explained by saying I want what He wants more than I want anything. What Jesus said in the garden, "Not my will, but thine be done." This is holiness. God's divine nature and will has absolute sway in our innermost being, so that His love compels us and motivates our actions and deeds. Blessed be the pure in heart, for they will see God. (Matthew 5:8)

God provides everything that we need for life and for godliness. Holiness is a process as well as a state of being, just like discipleship is a process as well as a state of being. Are you holy? Read that out loud and remember what Timothy wrote. We are not just told that we can say this but we are commanded to be this. Am I holy as He is holy? Am I set apart for His purpose? First you must be forgiven of sin, the acts that have stemmed from your selfish heart. Second, you must yield in word and deed to the Spirit of the Living God. Do not be a Christian who is forgiven, but still living life for you. There is freedom from the constant state of needing to repent because your heart continues to produce works that are sourced by self. Just like the prevenient grace of God pursued you revealing how much He loves you and wants to forgive you and make you His child, that same grace pursues you giving you the choice of your own will or His will for you. Have you yielded to Him? Are you willing? You do not need to understand it all or know what it means just now; He will work out all of those details and, believe me, the God of the universe is able to communicate to you if your ears are attentive to His voice. Here is a prayer that I pray from time to time to renew my vows so to speak with My God. Remember He does the work; all we do is willingly obey.

LORD, I give up all my own plans and purposes, all my own desires and hopes, and accept Your will for my life. I give myself, my time, my all, utterly to You to be Yours forever. Fill me and seal me with Your Holy Spirit. Use me as You will. Send me where You will. Orchestrate Your entire will in my life both now and forevermore. Amen.

Holiness is the end goal of the Groom for His Bride. The motive of my heart should be my love for God; and out of that love, I seek to do His will. This love compels me to not only righteousness, which is a right relationship with Him, but also to righteous acts, acts done out of a right relationship with Him.

Our Bridegroom is revealed to us and through us, but only to the extent that we love and obey Him. (John 15) It is His choice to reveal Himself in these days through His Church. The only way for us to talk of the Bridegroom is to talk of the love and subsequent surrender of the Bride to His nature and His way. Does my life yield to His Image without hindrance so that His Light shines through me?

Lord, deliver Your people from ourselves and glorify Yourself through us. Overwhelm us as you put Your love in our hearts. You make all things beautiful in Your time.

Chapter Three

The Bride of Christ

Sometimes the language that we use in the church is used so much that we have a hint of understanding, but because we understand, we do not continue the search to understand more. So it is with most people in looking at the bride of Christ. There is much symbolism in the Jewish marriage ceremony and how that relates to the relationship between Christ and the Church. There are instructions in the letters of the New Testament that are for husbands and wives, that seem to be primarily directed to the human equivalent of marriage, that reveals a little more information about Christ and the Church. We are limited in any illustration used to explain God, His Character or His relationship to us. What can explain the unexplainable? So as we look at marriage and the relationship between husband and wife from the scriptures, the goal of what Paul or Solomon is writing is always to reveal God using limited circumstances and explanations. While the Bible talks about marriage, it is important to note that the explanation of marriage is to explain or reveal God, not vice versa. So even though Paul writes in Ephesians 5:32, "This mystery is profound, and I am saying that it refers to Christ and the church.", this is not an afterthought in his expose about marriage but rather a digression into marriage trying to help his readers understand the relationship between Christ and His people.

So let's begin at the end, since the marriage is the one thing that gives the Bride her name, her identity and her hope. John writes from the isle of Patmos in Revelation 19:7-8:

"Let us rejoice and exult
and give him the glory,
For the marriage of the Lamb has come,
And his Bride has made herself ready;
It was granted her to clothe herself
With fine linen, bright and pure—
For the fine linen is the righteous deeds of the saints."

Beginning here gives us perspective and even a process that is revealed in the form of calling in the New Testament and symbols in the Old Testament.

There is a marriage that will take place to fulfill the word of God. This marriage will be between Jesus Christ, the Lamb of God, and the Bride, which Paul tells us in his letter to Ephesus, is the Church. To know that someday our faith will be our sight and we will be in the presence of our Prince of Peace, when we will see clearly and know clearly, where there will be no more pain and no more crying, that is the eyes of faith taking a deep breath for endurance and strength.

This passage offers another perspective that is essential to be able to grab on to during the discouraging legs of this journey as Christians, and especially as leaders. You know those times, at least for me when everywhere I look I see the scripture verse, "Do not grow weary in well doing, for in due time you will reap a harvest, if you faint not." I do not know where this passage of scripture is found without looking it up, but I did not even hesitate in typing it out. It has been well worn in my life. In fact this is my cue scripture. When I see it, I check my journey and see where I may need to guard and prepare for a long haul. During that preparation, the perspective that Revelation brings to me is this: the Bride will be ready. I know that you would say here, duh, of course, but read it carefully: how is she made ready? She has on the fine linen. If you ask the question to anyone theologically minded, without using this particular scripture but rather wording it like, "How is the body of Christ made ready for His coming?" you would get an answer like, "Christ has made her ready." But look at it again. The fine linen is the righteous deeds of the saints that made the Bride ready... uhhh.... okay, who are the saints? Is that synonymous with the Church? You know, those that are forgiven of their sins? I could simply say no, but I want you to get this.

There is a distinction of our works made by Paul in his second letter to Timothy. He talks of the vessel that produces work that is for regular use, but after the vessel is purified, or rather set apart for noble purposes, then all works that are consistent with these purposes are useful to the master. This idea of being set apart for special use is the definition for holy. So while there are some people who love Jesus and are on a journey of faith, where Christ is their Savior, they may have not reached the point of being crucified with Christ so that they are no longer acting and living life unto themselves, but rather they yield their will to the will of the Father. Deeds done in the body, in this life, are pure not because they are good or bad in and of themselves but because of the will or motive behind them. I can encourage someone out of flattery or out of love and spurring them on. It is the motive which counts. So works that are pure or rather come from a saint, one who is

24

holy or set apart for God, are the things that make up the fine linen that clothes the Bride of Christ.

Now do not think that I am saying that the wedding dress is only the righteous deeds of those set apart to be leaders. These deeds are the righteous acts of the saints, everyone is called to be holy as God is holy; these are the righteous acts of the people of God.

All of the planning for a wedding is done and the climax or biggest moment of the entire ceremony other than the kiss is the entrance. It is the moment that the music starts, the groom turns, the family and friends on both sides rise. The bridesmaids remain in the place they have been since they proceeded down the aisle making the way with petals and precedence. They are waiting. All are waiting. The door opens and everyone is a gasp at how beautiful this Bride is who at this point is completely covered from head to toe in, you guessed it, the dress.

These righteous acts of the saints which are now hidden away from sight as they are woven together and made beautiful. These acts are already done in the world before the wedding. They are the deeds done in the body that are of gold and of silver worth. These are the acts that will be seen together to make up the outward adornment of the Bride. The jewels in the crowns, so to speak, of the Church that will be brought before the Lamb of God, our Bridegroom.

Please know that the Bride of Christ is not as some in the church realm see it, the second rate citizen while the leaders, pastors, teachers are on display for all to applaud and see. That is not biblical. Preaching, yes, teaching, yes, and other things leaders are called to do that may put them in front of those they influence, but it is the righteous acts of the

Bride of Christ that are to be knitted together to form the unity in the name of Jesus that brings glory to Him alone. So many times things get upside down. We forget why we are here.

Why are we all, the Body of Christ here? The Body of Christ is here to give a taste of the Spirit of the Living God who dwells within us to a world in darkness. We are here to reveal the kingdom of Light so that people may see and have opportunity to turn from their life of sin and darkness to Him who knew no sin so they can be forgiven and walk in the Light. This is done through our good works that they see which draws their attention to the One who is the Source of the love which motivates our actions. (Matthew 5)

While we understand weddings in this way, there is a little insight that the Jewish customs for marriage reveal. The Bridesmaids attend to the Bride in her own house while the Bridegroom prepares the place where they will live. This could take up to a year. While waiting, the bride-to-be gets ready by learning how to be a wife and how to please her groom to be. When he comes to receive his bride, there is great celebration and rejoicing.

This preparation of learning how to be a wife and learning how to please her husband certainly is similar to Hebrew 13:20-21, "May the God of peace, who through the blood of the eternal covenant brought back from the dead our Lord Jesus, that great Shepherd of the sheep, equip you with everything good for doing His will, and may He work in us what is pleasing to Him, through Jesus Christ, to whom be glory for ever and ever. Amen."

With these truths about the Church, the Bride of Christ, it is understood what we are here to do. Good works that God prepared in advance for us to do from a pure heart that is forgiven and made holy or set apart for His good pleasure. Without faith, it is impossible to please the Lord. Without holiness no one will see the Lord. So as His Bride, may we all walk by faith and not by sight; may we yield our lives to the will of the One who laid His life down for us so that we will be made ready, glorifying our coming King so that as we lift Him up, others will be drawn by His Spirit to know Him and make Him known.

Chapter Four

The Call of a Bridesmaid

Perhaps you remember the Carol Burnett Show and her most famous sketch mimicking "Gone with the Wind". In the original movie, Scarlett had become resourceful during hard times and made a very nice dress from the drapery in the Tara Plantation Home before going to see Rhett and asking for money. Well Carol Burnett, who played Scarlett in this spoof, came down the stairs looking like she had just taken the drapery off the window and placed it on her shoulders, curtain rod and all. When I think about this fine linen that is the picture I get. The material is there, at least in the end. In order for the Bride to be clothed in it, much needs to happen. There must be measuring, cutting, preparing, sewing, pressing, fitting, trimming, taping, pinning, and then wearing. So who does all of this? Well in a real wedding people do not ask that question, and in this wedding that is not the emphasis in the end. The emphasis is exactly where it should be - on the Bride and Groom. But all of this did happen and it was the Bridesmaids that saw that it got done.

There is a call to be a bridesmaid and a call to make the Church ready, not just to the extent of the Church being the Church in the world but to the extent of ministering to the Bride. Ephesians chapter 4 is the one chapter that tells us the breakdown of God's will for those that minister to the Bride. In Ephesians 4:1-13, Paul writes:

I, therefore, the prisoner for the Lord, urge you to live worthily of the calling with which you have been called, with all humility and gentleness, with patience, bearing with one another in love, making every effort to keep the unity of the Spirit in the bond of peace. There is one body and one Spirit, just as you too were called to the one hope of your calling, one Lord, one faith, one baptism, one God and Father of all, who is over all and through all and in all.

But to each one of us grace was given according to the measure of the gift of Christ. Therefore it says, "When he ascended on high he captured captives; he gave gifts to men." Now what is the meaning of "he ascended," except that he also descended to the lower regions, namely, the earth? He, the very one who descended, is also the one who ascended above all the heavens, in order to fill all things. It was he who gave some as apostles, some as prophets, some as evangelists, and some as pastors and teachers, to equip the saints for the work of ministry, that is, to build up the body of Christ, until we all attain to the unity of the faith and of the knowledge of the Son of God – a mature person, attaining to the measure of Christ's full stature.

Note that the gifts that God gives to the Bride of Christ are the actual people that fulfill the callings of apostles, prophets, evangelists, pastors and teachers. We will look at each gift individually to see the purpose and fulfilling of the will of God as the Bride receives the gifts and ministries given.

Before we explain these gifts that are given, we need to make the distinction between these gifts which are given to people whom God has specifically called, and the gifts the entire body receives according to the Spirit. There are people who are appointed as administrators, deacons and elders within the church. Paul writes later in 1 Timothy and other letters about the deacons that are called and how they should live, being the husband of one wife and other distinctions that show that they are people of integrity. I know that there is debate in the church about women being in some of these positions. However, I believe that if we look at these roles realistically and what they entail, we may find that we are completely persuaded already having women serve as deacons in the church; in fact, while they may not hold the title, they hold the responsibility. In the day that Paul was writing these words, the culture lived in a society of hierarchy, where they really did not understand democracy or working things through from a consensus. In an authoritative structure, you need a manager or administrator that can come in and speak the people's language by laying it down on the line. This is the strength of male leadership. Now you may find in our culture those that manage come in and talk things through by hearing people out and coming to a conclusion that is explained and well thought out, so that we can have a general positive consensus which appeals to the entire counsel of ideas. This is the strength of female leadership.

This story helps me to decipher the difference between this deacon or administrator role and the role of pastor. We had a funeral to officiate at one of the churches where I was on staff. The other female pastor was working with a couple of other pastors to make the arrangements and order of service with the funeral director and the family. A few friends of the family who were not aware of the normal process of our church staff became involved in making more arrangements and changing things around. While there was no ill intent here and most were not aware of what was happening, we had an administrative collision of plans that had to be ironed out. The female pastor came into the middle of the situation and had to administrate and manage the situation. In a conversation later with her I asked her what she thought would have been different if one of the male pastors had walked in. She said that they would have come in and pretty clearly said this is what we have planned and this is the way that we have worked it out. I have no doubt they would have done that full of grace and love, but they would have laid down the facts and those involved would have graciously and reverently accepted the process. However, the way this pastor handled the situation was different because she came in and listened to what they had to say, pulled the plan together and modified the process of the church to accommodate the request as best as possible, while still maintaining the routine of the staff that was already in process. Not wrong, just different. Either way the funeral was wonderful and meaningful and full of ministry and love. Whether it was because of whom she was or because she knew the response to her would be different, she took a more diplomatic approach.

In Paul's culture, a female could not be a deacon or administrator for a couple of reasons. Not only did women more than likely not have the education to do the job, but probably more importantly, women did not have the respect in that society to influence the people in an effective way. I do not want to make male and female roles the issue while discussing and discovering the gifts that God has given, but I do want to make the distinction between this role and the roles mentioned in Ephesians. The book of Acts probably reveals this role best, in chapter 6:1-7, where Luke mentions that the apostles did not have time to wait on tables (serve the crowds) but needed to devote themselves to the study of the Word. At that point the disciples elected seven deacons full of the Holy Spirit.

Moving forward into the servant leadership roles that are gifts to the Church, we are image bearers for our King to represent Him and allow Him to minister through us. These gifts are gifts not necessarily to manage the Body of Christ, but to inspire, to spur on, to inform them on how to walk in love and obedience and holiness. These five kinds of gifts are given to the Bride, and as I said before, the gifts are not inanimate objects but actual people, vessels that God uses and raises up to be apostles, prophets, evangelists, pastors and teachers. Their purpose in its totality is told to us in Ephesians 4:12-13; they are "to equip the saints for the work of ministry, that is, to build up the body of Christ, until we all attain to the unity of the faith and of the knowledge of the Son of God – a mature person, attaining to the measure of Christ's full stature."

Apostles refers to those who saw Jesus face to face, heard from Jesus one on one, and is now revealing the doctrine and Truth of the Way to the Church. That is why apostleship is so important in our church history. When our founding fathers of the faith met to discuss the New Testament and what letters and books would be considered the Word of the Living God, they had certain criteria necessary for a book to be included in the canon. First they were looking for people who could give us firsthand accounts. This eyewitness account is essential for the passing down of our faith. The apostles keep us close to the root. The Greek word for apostle is (read aloud with me) "αποστολοσ", (good) which means "sent out one", "messenger", or "one sent out with orders".

Next I want to explore the gift of evangelist because it is so closely associated with apostle. Evangelist from its root means "bringer of good tidings". The New Testament refers to those that carry the message of the Gospel of salvation to the world. While the apostles received this command, evangelists are those that take the command from the testimony of the apostles and carry the message of Truth to the ends of the earth. The Gospel is spread throughout the world by messengers who are given to a group of people to tell the good news. The first evangelists were Mary Magdalene, Mary the Mother of Jesus and Salome the mother of James, son of Zebedee. According to the Gospels, they were at the tomb on Resurrection morning where Jesus appeared to them and told them to go and tell the disciples and Peter that He is risen. Please think this through with me because even as I type it I can hear the responses, but by the definition of apostleship, these same women could also be called apostles. Simply put, an evangelist is someone who has a burden or a passion to go and tell people about Jesus. A true evangelist believes that if they tell people the good news of the Gospel then people will respond. They do not have a thought, just like those ladies that day running from the tomb who were not believed at first, they did not even think twice, about whether or not the disciples would believe or accept their testimony. That was not their concern or their thought process. So an evangelist has this ultimate positive perspective too. They subscribe to the notion that as long as people hear with open ears, and I will tell until they hear, then how could they not receive Him? What passion? They know they have the words of life and they are adamant about spreading the message.

I was having lunch with a friend of mine and we were discussing what we have a passion for. I am a passionate person and while explaining my heart as best I could, we began to explore the part that passion and zeal play in the purpose that God has for our lives. We began to talk about how the passion that we have really does stem from the zeal that God has to accomplish His will through us. I began to realize that I used to have a passion for teaching children, but now my passion is burning from a slightly different perspective because I have a passion for the parents and other leaders that influence people for the next generation. I believe that God allows us to feel His passion according to the role that we are serving in the Church. My friend began to explain how she used to have a passion for training leaders, but now she has a passion for administration. Then I asked her the question that we both knew the answer to, "What is your current ministry position?" and of course it is administration. God blesses His children with His Spirit and His zeal according to their purpose. I believe that as this passion begins to change, we should keep our ears open to see what part of His zeal He needs represented from that. It is very frustrating to be doing one thing, but have a passion for another thing.

I used to believe that the prophet was the one who would stand up and shock and awe people with a message from God. However, the prophet has always been the representation of the wisdom of God, the mercy or judgment of God. This prophet has been given to the Church, so that the Church would have an idea of what the Bridegroom would say. The actual Greek root here means "foreteller" or "to say before". We believe that the Holy Spirit speaks to His people and that the sheep know the Shepherd's voice; however, there is a time as every believer grows and matures that they have to learn how to discern the voice and will of God. As God becomes Savior to those born again, the prophet serves as a bridge to people hearing the Holy Spirit. It is not that they can't, it's just that they don't know which voice to follow. It is like a dog learning to obey the master. The dog needs to train to know not only the voice of the master but also the word of the master. The prophet's responsibility is to help the people of God hear the voice of God. God puts His Spirit within the prophet and gives them wisdom so that the people see and recognize the wisdom of God with skin on. This seeking and learning how to hear the voice of God is best learned in Holy Spiritual Community. I have in the past gone to one who, after being around them, I know I can ask them about how I would discern God's will in a situation. The prophet walks through a problem or a question filled with the discernment of God. There are prophets who stood up for the word and wisdom of God in the Old Testament like Jeremiah, Deborah, and Samuel. These prophets whether they were heeded or not were God's gift to the people of Israel. The Prophet of God knows the will of God because the Spirit of God dwells within him or her, and they through experience and longevity hear Him. The Prophet is a specific person who is given to the Body.

My pastor ended the last board meeting by helping the leaders of our church to understand this role of prophet. So much so that he had to stop after saying what he said and tell the people point blank, "I am speaking in the role of prophet right now. I have never been that blunt in speaking the words of God, but you as leaders need to understand that I speak this not of my own thoughts, but this is indeed the heart of the Spirit of God and the direction of His will." I have never in my years there heard our pastor be so specific; however, I will say that the next words out of his mouth were the third confirmation for me that this was what God was saying to us as a church and to the church in America. I know you are wondering what he said and while I cannot repeat exactly, basically God is waking His Church. So wake up! This was not only an insight into the heart of God, but also a call to obedience. God is speaking and the prophet is echoing.

The next gifts mentioned are adjoined, pastors and teachers, but I want to look at them separately. While I believe these gifts work in tandem with each other very closely, hence the adjunction, it is important that we understand the difference between the two.

Another word for pastor is shepherd. The early church understood this concept without explanation. Shepherds were a part of their culture. Most shepherds were the youngest or even the young girls of the family. The pastor of a church, a community, or a family is the one who has been there a while. They know the people and the people know them. That is how Jesus described himself when He talked about being the Good Shepherd. He said that the sheep know His voice. So a pastor is among the people in holy spiritual community, not over it, not as an add-on, but truly a part of this holy spiritual community, realizing that the Good Shepherd is the only one over all the sheep. The shepherd is trusted and looked to in administering spiritual nutrition and care of the people. The pastor as shepherd is truly walking with the people. They are not a flash-in-the-pan presence with a word of God. While the pastor is given by God to shepherd the people, a pastor may not be the actual weekly pulpit preacher, even though in our culture we make this assumption. On the other hand, we have a pastor who is not on staff that we call an evangelist at our church. Because he walks closely as a mentor with our pastor and *comes to minister to us* once or twice a year, he has become another shepherd to our fold because of his longevity and transparency. We love him like family and we entrust our spiritual care in part to him… a shepherd for the Shepherd.

While pastors minister with compassion to the people and administer grace themselves, or through other people, so that the love of Christ is shed abroad through the body and the grace of Christ abounds, the teacher is different. Remember the gift is the teacher, not the information. Jesus would preach to the multitudes as evangelist or prophet, but he would then go over the parables again with His disciples by asking them if they got it. When they said they didn't, He would then explain it to them again until they got it. He did not give more than they could handle in teaching, while in contrast he would blanket preach parables to those who could not understand so that the seed would be awakened and taught later to them. The teacher makes sure to reconcile the understanding of the hearer so that that truth is understood as much as possible. The teacher wants to unpack and explain the truth so that, in the student's human intellect and the spiritual teaching of the Holy Spirit, they are able to connect the dots and make sense of it. This is not necessarily common sense but rather a reconciliation of the spiritual truth and their practical walk. While the pastor looks at the people they may know and sees need with compassion and ministers in that vein, the teacher sees the potential with hope and ministers in that vein.

Pastors and teachers walk with the people. Apostles, Prophets and Evangelists walk to the people. Paul encourages us in Ephesians to walk in a manner worthy of the calling that we have received. While we are sheep, we are also gifts to the bride of Christ. So whether you are Jew or Greek, male or female, stand up in the calling you have received from God. Realizing that we are called by His grace, not because of who we are, but because of who He is. He gave His best, Himself. Let us not forget it is Him who works through us to build up the Church. God is no respecter of persons; He only works through a yielded vessel.

Chapter Five

The Ear of a Bridesmaid

Dear Heavenly Father,

Thank You for how very relevant Your Word is today. Thank You God for speaking into the circumstances of Your people. Thank You that You are the Alpha and the Omega, the beginning and the end and that Your Word never returns void. Lord, I ask You to reveal truth and to give me, and those following along with me, wisdom and depth of insight so that we may know You more, and that we may be full of Your Spirit so that we can be effective in not only displaying and making You known but in loving You and loving each other. Lord, as the famous song says, "I want what You want more than I want anything." So, Father, I pray that You would give me the heart of a yielded Bridesmaid and that You would glorify yourself because if You are glorified, then I am satisfied. In Jesus' Name. Amen.

Jesus, the revealed Word, preaches and teaches throughout the gospels using parables. Many times Jesus is speaking not only to His disciples but also to the multitudes. On the Mount of Olives along the Sea of Galilee, He is teaching about the future and many other things. There are three parables that Matthew writes down from His teaching in Matthew chapters 24 and 25. We can glean meaning and allow God to reveal His wisdom and depth of insight from these parables, not only as His people but more importantly as leaders and equippers of the people of God. The introduction to these parables from the New International Version begins in verse 24:36.

> 36 "But about that day or hour no one knows, not even the angels in heaven, nor the Son, but only the Father. 37 As it was in the days of Noah, so it will be at the coming of the Son of Man. 38 For in the days before the flood, people were eating and drinking, marrying and giving in marriage, up to the day Noah entered the ark; 39 and they knew nothing about what would happen until the flood came and took them all away. That is how it will be at the coming of the Son of Man. 40 Two men will be in the field; one will be taken and the other left. 41 Two women will be grinding with a hand mill; one will be taken and the other left.
> 42 "Therefore keep watch, because you do not know on what day your Lord will come. 43 But understand this: If the owner of the house had known at what time of night the thief was coming, he would have kept watch and would not have let his house be broken into. 44 So you also must be ready, because the Son of Man will come at an hour when you do not expect him.
> 45 "Who then is the faithful and wise servant, whom the master has put in charge of the servants in his household to give them their food at the proper time? 46 It will be good for that servant whose master finds him doing so when he returns. 47 Truly I tell you, he will put him in charge of all his possessions. 48 But suppose that servant is wicked and says to himself, 'My master is staying away a long time,' 49 and he then begins to beat his fellow servants and to eat and drink with drunkards. 50 The master of that servant will come on a day when he does not expect him and at an hour he is not aware of. 51 He will cut him to pieces and assign him a place with the hypocrites, where there will be weeping and gnashing of teeth.

While there are many theologies and debates about this passage of scripture, for our purposes, let's examine who Jesus is talking to and who Jesus is talking about. In verse 44, who is the "you" He is talking about? We know the actual audience, but He explains a little more in the subsequent verses about the kind of people He is talking about.

Jesus is talking to those who have ears, who are His sheep, but it is more than that. When you talk to a group of people about themselves, for instance a group of siblings or a team, while you are speaking to the team and the children, you really are giving the leaders, the eldest or the captain information to be used while you are gone. The same thing is happening here. Jesus is talking to His people about His people. So in essence, He is talking to the leaders of His people. With those ears attentive, let's look at the next verse. It makes sense that in the next verse you would find a description of these leaders. "Who then is the faithful and wise servant, whom the master has put in charge of the servants in his household to give them their food at the proper time?" Jesus is called faithful and true, full of wisdom and knowledge, He who came to serve. Would it not also be that He would call the leaders who are to lead His people to do the same. So He is separating out the Bride of Christ from those who would be attending to the Bride, the Church from those that would take care of the body of Christ.

It is very interesting the three words that Jesus used to describe the ones who are put in charge. He is not talking to every individual, but rather to the leaders. He calls them "faithful and wise servant". This is the only situation that we find in these verses that a person will be held responsible for other people. In James 3:5, James warns us, "Not many of you should presume to be teachers, my brothers, because you know that we who teach will be judged more strictly." So those that are in authority in the realm of the church are to be a certain way and if they are not, they are responsible for the repercussions of their actions. We, as leaders, are called to be faithful, wise servants. Our works will be judged by that rod. Jesus continued as he told parables to describe these words more clearly.

The first parable that Jesus tells the people, after addressing them and calling attention to those who would be in charge of other servants, is found in Matthew 25. Watch how He again reiterates on the adjectives used to describe those left in charge. This is the same word, 'phronimos', meaning wise, which He used in the previous paragraph. It is as if He is explaining how to be wise to those who have the ears of leaders.

[1] "At that time the kingdom of heaven will be like ten virgins who took their lamps and went out to meet the bridegroom. [2] Five of them were foolish and five were wise. [3] The foolish ones took their lamps but did not take any oil with them. [4] The wise ones, however, took oil in jars along with their lamps. [5] The bridegroom was a long time in coming, and they all became drowsy and fell asleep.

[6] "At midnight the cry rang out: 'Here's the bridegroom! Come out to meet him!'

[7] "Then all the virgins woke up and trimmed their lamps. [8] The foolish ones said to the wise, 'Give us some of your oil; our lamps are going out.'

[9] "'No,' they replied, 'there may not be enough for both us and you. Instead, go to those who sell oil and buy some for yourselves.'

[10] "But while they were on their way to buy the oil, the bridegroom arrived. The virgins who were ready went in with him to the wedding banquet. And the door was shut.

[11] "Later the others also came. 'Lord, Lord,' they said, 'open the door for us!'

[12] "But he replied, 'Truly I tell you, I don't know you.'

[13] "Therefore keep watch, because you do not know the day or the hour.'"

In this parable about virgins, which in the Word alludes to those who have been made clean by the blood of the Lamb, we can understand that this is corporately the bride herself that Jesus speaks of. The word virgin includes them in the number made clean, however in context of the previous passage we understand that it is the state of being wise or foolish that separates these virgins. Within the context, it makes sense that these are not just the bride but the bridesmaids or ladies in waiting who attend to the bride. While they are waiting for the Bridegroom with or without oil, if they are just concerned with themselves as one escaping from the flames, then what of the oil? The oil suggests that the provision they have is not enough. In leadership terms, you may have heard it referred to as "change in your pocket", or literally influence over those you lead. The foolish virgins gave up their influence over those they lead. While they may have kept up appearances, in the end it was not enough even for them. I know this is not the conventional interpretation of the oil being the Holy Spirit, but think again about the wise and foolish adjectives here. Realizing that all ten virgins were waiting on the Bridegroom and all ten virgins were indeed virgins. The only difference here is that in waiting for the Bridegroom the foolish ones left their post at a crucial time. They did not keep watch as described in Matthew 24:42-43 when talking about the owner of a house or the leader of servants. They did not count the cost before taking their place as leader or lady in waiting. They came up short. This leads right into our next parable.

The parable of the loaned money also expounds on the adjective used for the faithful and wise servant. Here the servants are separated out according to their faithfulness to the Master.

¹⁴ "Again, it will be like a man going on a journey, who called his servants and entrusted his wealth to them. ¹⁵ To one he gave five bags of gold, to another two bags, and to another one bag, each according to his ability. Then he went on his journey. ¹⁶ The man who had received five bags of gold went at once and put his money to work and gained five bags more. ¹⁷ So also, the one with two bags of gold gained two more. ¹⁸ But the man who had received one bag went off, dug a hole in the ground and hid his master's money.

¹⁹ "After a long time the master of those servants returned and settled accounts with them. ²⁰ The man who had received five bags of gold brought the other five. 'Master,' he said, 'you entrusted me with five bags of gold. See, I have gained five more.'

²¹ "His master replied, 'Well done, good and faithful servant! You have been faithful with a few things; I will put you in charge of many things. Come and share your master's happiness!'

²² "The man with two bags of gold also came. 'Master,' he said, 'you entrusted me with two bags of gold; see, I have gained two more.'

²³ "His master replied, 'Well done, good and faithful servant! You have been faithful with a few things; I will put you in charge of many things. Come and share your master's happiness!'

²⁴ "Then the man who had received one bag of gold came. 'Master,' he said, 'I knew that you are a hard man, harvesting where you have not sown and gathering where you have not scattered seed. ²⁵ So I was afraid and went out and hid your gold in the ground. See, here is what belongs to you.'

²⁶ "His master replied, 'You wicked, lazy servant! So you knew that I harvest where I have not sown and gather where I have not scattered seed? ²⁷ Well then, you should have put my money on deposit with the bankers, so that when I returned I would have received it back with interest.

²⁸ "'So take the bag of gold from him and give it to the one who has ten bags. ²⁹ For whoever has will be given more, and they will have an abundance. Whoever does not have, even what they have will be taken from them. ³⁰ And throw that worthless

servant outside, into the darkness, where there will be weeping and gnashing of teeth.'

No matter the outcome of the servants that invested the money that was left, they were faithful. Jesus said to the first servant, "well done good and faithful servant", and He also said to the second servant, "well done good and faithful servant". Their reward was increased influence and they were told to come and share their master's happiness, in some translations, it reads, enter into the joy of the Lord. Then the man who received the one talent explained what he thought of the master and what he did with the bag of gold. Interestingly enough the master reiterates what the wicked servant believed about him.

In both of these parables it seems that the master returned and was dissatisfied by works. Why is it that we look and we see that there is severe judgment based on works in the age of grace where we are saved by faith? Our Lord is telling us if we are leaders, we call ourselves leaders, we are responsible and we influence the faith of others and how they see God. We hold in our hands eternity in the lives of men and women around us. What a grave responsibility. James reminds us that we see our faith by our works. Therefore if we call ourselves leaders and our works do not inspire and spur on those we lead, then our faith or lack thereof has become a stumbling block to others. There is much to say about one who leads someone astray or becomes a stumbling block. However there is one other nugget of truth here that we cannot overlook.

We as leaders sometimes think that it is appalling to leave our post or forsake those we lead by stepping down or going on extended leave or even going on a sabbatical. We see this as failure or at best laziness. However, in this parable of the talents, the master says to the wicked servant that he would have been faithful had he at least put the money on loan to the bank. The other servants did not share what they thought of the master, but the wicked one did, almost like making an excuse as to why there was not increase or growth. If we find ourselves there as leaders, that is a good sign; we are ready to loan our influence to another leader and allow ourselves to be adjusted by the Master. So, we can look and glean from these parables what Christ has called us to, a joy description.

One other point to discuss is the difference between a legalist interpretation and a holiness interpretation. A legalist might say that as leaders we should be very dogmatic, because in preparation for when God comes back to judge our works we have to continually go over them and make sure that we are counting the cost and doing our part. A holiness interpretation would say Christ has come that we would be set free, even for leaders. Free from what? Free from the yoke. His yoke is easy and His burden is light. So how can we be free from the yoke, the expectation of what we are to be? Holiness is the answer. While this is a poorly defined word in some circles, let me reiterate what I mean when I say holiness. Holiness simply means a vessel yielded, set apart, surrendered to the Spirit of the Living God. A vessel where we are experiencing a relationship of intimacy and rest, where we can lean into the heart and heartbeat of God and trust that, as we walk in obedience, He is guiding us into all wisdom. The lazy and wicked servant explained what he saw of the master. Because he withdrew from God, his viewpoint of who the Master is became skewed. In reality, when we withdraw and no longer are sourced by the Spirit of the Living God as leaders, then our perspective becomes skewed and we have a form or outward appearance of godliness but deny the power thereof. On the other hand, if the Spirit of the Living God is spreading the seed and growing the seed through the servant, then the reality of who God is continues to reveal His character not only to His faithful and wise servant but through him or her as well.

The last parable is very well known. It is called the Sheep and the Goats. Songs have been written about this separation of people that stands in stark difference from the saved by grace mentality, but adds the works aspect to this saving faith.

Matthew 25:31-46

[31] "When the Son of Man comes in his glory, and all the angels with him, he will sit on his glorious throne. [32] All the nations will be gathered before him, and he will separate the people one from another as a shepherd separates the sheep from the goats. [33] He will put the sheep on his right and the goats on his left.

[34] "Then the King will say to those on his right, 'Come, you who are blessed by my Father; take your inheritance, the kingdom prepared for you since the creation of the world. [35] For I was hungry and you gave me something to eat, I was thirsty and you gave me something to drink, I was a stranger and you invited me in, [36] I needed clothes and you clothed me, I was sick and you looked after me, I was in prison and you came to visit me.'

[37] "Then the righteous will answer him, 'Lord, when did we see you hungry and feed you, or thirsty and give you something to drink? [38] When did we see you a stranger and invite you in or needing clothes and clothe you? [39] When did we see you sick or in prison and go to visit you?'

[40] "The King will reply, 'Truly I tell you, whatever you did for one of the least of these brothers and sisters of mine, you did for me.'

[41] "Then he will say to those on his left, 'Depart from me, you who are cursed, into the eternal fire prepared for the devil and his angels. [42] For I was hungry and you gave me nothing to eat, I was thirsty and you gave me nothing to drink, [43] I was a stranger and you did not invite me in, I needed clothes and you did not clothe me, I was sick and in prison and you did not look after me.'

[44] "They also will answer, 'Lord, when did we see you hungry or thirsty or a stranger or needing clothes or sick or in prison, and did not help you?'

[45] "He will reply, 'Truly I tell you, whatever you did not do for one of the least of these, you did not do for me.'

[46] "Then they will go away to eternal punishment, but the righteous to eternal life."

I have always thought, "Lord that is a little harsh, don't you think?" God has helped me in looking at this scripture, since I cannot remember doing some of these things specifically or individually. However as I have walked as a leader alongside other leaders, an equipper amidst other equippers, I heard as an echo in my mind the word "you"... "For I was hungry and 'you' gave me something to eat". The word "you" is plural there. And maybe the meaning of this parable for the leader is to understand that we are little shepherds who have influence over sheep. We have decisions and responsibilities to and over sheep to guide them, equip them, teach them, and show them how to live and to make them ready for the bridegroom to come. We do this by doing exactly what Christ has commanded us to do. Throughout the New Testament we see the Church is called in the name of Jesus to feed the hungry, invite the stranger in, look after the sick, orphans and widows. Yes, we are called to preach the gospel, and that we do well, but have we equipped the body of Christ to care and love so that Christ may be seen in and through them? "And they will know we are His disciples by the way we love each other."

As Jesus is talking to the sheep and goats, He is talking to leaders. Sure He is talking to all of them, but the ones with the ears are the team leaders. So while I may not go to prison, if there is someone under my influence that I can equip and encourage to go to the prison, then I should influence their heart so that it beats with the heartbeat of God and go to those in prison. Yes, this is the call and the investment to prepare a bride that is reaching out in the name of Jesus. To be able to influence the vision and craft the heartbeat, so that the bride can catch His heart not only through His word but also through the influence of those in leadership in their lives.

Pastor Todd, a Church of the Nazarene pastor in Virginia took the words of Jesus to heart. Here are his words and how they have implemented this call in the local church,

"I, like many other pastors, tended to work within the historical and cultural parameters set by the local church context. And I, like many pastors, experienced a mixture of safety and frustration. What was missing was any significant heartbeat for the practical needs of those outside the church. "Why should we buy their groceries or pay their bills when they waste so much money on cigarettes and alcohol?" Of course this objection never, ever touched on any of the ways that we within the church waste money! The Lord began working in secret, preparing a few hearts to receive his Word. As that was happening He opened Matthew 25:31-46 in a new way to my own heart. The inescapable necessity of doing works of

49

gracious mercy became clear. The tone of this teaching shouted out - "Do these and you're in; don't and you're out." Not only are these works necessary to those who receive them - and Jesus said that He was the recipient! - But they are necessary for those who do them. From this new conviction "The Top Five of Jesus" was born. As this was taught and talked about it took root in the hearts that the Lord had been preparing. This "Top Five" - feeding the hungry, giving drink to the thirsty, clothing the needy, showing hospitality to strangers and ministering to the sick and imprisoned - has become one of our top goals and one of our guiding principles. And it is working!

'Oh, the earlier objection about helping those who waste money? My standard reply is this: "Aren't you glad God did not require you to clean up your bad habits before He extended grace to you?"

These parables provide many truths, not only to the individual to be faithful and wise, but I believe that God is speaking directly to those of us who lead, those of us who are called to equip, those of us who are called to encourage, those of us who have influence. If you are grappling with the calling, good, you should be. If you have not grappled with the call to lead, I question the call because this is not a place of honor or a place to be above, but rather we answer the call out of love for and obedience to Christ. If anything else is on the table, then the cost is too high for what you are shooting for. Christ calls us to be His faithful and wise servant. With this sobering outlook and these sobering passages on what we are called to be then pride, ability, and false humility have no place; only obedience to the call, boldness with the message, and courage with the consequences and the cost. So will you journey with me to explore what it means to be a bridesmaid, a faithful and wise servant, a little shepherd whose eyes are fixed on the Good Shepherd? Obedience is better than sacrifice, but as a leader sacrifice is just one of the costs of obedience. Because we love Him we will journey together with Jesus as our Focus, our Capstone, our King, our Bridegroom.

Chapter Six

Here come the Bridesmaids…

One day I was surfing the net and came upon the article that inspired this book whose namesake is this chapter. I had recently been a bridesmaid in my brother's wedding which was beautiful, and I was wearing one of my favorite colors, pink. I was older and there was slightly more of me than the rest of the bridesmaids, but there has to be one, right? ☺ Anyway, I found this article by Abigail Green online and began to read and assess what kind of bridesmaid I was. I found my mind wandering in several different directions because of my devotional time over the past few days. John the Revelator talks about the bride of Christ in Revelation 19. I thought about the wedding that would far outweigh anything that we could present on earth. Then I thought about the bridesmaids. We will look at this concept in greater depth, but understand that we, the pastors, teachers, prophets, evangelists and apostles are the bridesmaids. Don't go pious on me like my mind is trying to do. I realize that each believer is individually responsible for making the choice to follow Christ and for their own faith. I realize that it is Christ who dwells in each of us to work and do His good will. However, in this realm of Holy Christian Community where we spur each other on and iron sharpens iron, I think it is beneficial to look at this wonderful article and see how the easy pitfalls of regular bridesmaids, who "fill the velour fabric industry with profit", line up with the bridesmaids that may not be as fancily dressed but certainly still have a purpose to fulfill. Abigail introduces us to the reality of life for a bridesmaid, "As bridesmaids, they'll throw you a shower, plan a bachelorette bash and attend other pre-wedding events, **which means you'll be spending a good deal of time** with them in the coming months. But weddings have a way of **bringing out people's true colors**." I wanted to keep all of her sentences so you could see them in context, but look at the reality of the situation. You as a leader, as a bridesmaid, will spend a good deal of time with the Bride and this will bring out your true colors. In my life this has certainly been true. When my purpose and my plan collide with God's plan for His people, which then collides with the plan and purpose of all of the Bride of Christ that also have free will, wow, what a recipe for heartfelt emotions to be brought to the surface. Now let's look at the line up with this in mind. When you look at these and begin to measure others or to measure yourself, stop and ask God to forgive you. His perspective is all that matters and these are meant, as my pastor says, to minimize future regret, not condemn the past.

Scripture Meditation:

Mark 9:42 - "These little ones believe in me. It would be best for the person who causes one of them to lose faith to be thrown into the sea with a large stone hung around his neck."
James 3:1 - "Brothers and sisters, not many of you should become teachers. You know that we who teach will be judged more severely."

> Lord, make me like You, make me like You, You were a servant make me one too. Lord I am willing do what You must do…to make me like You Lord, make me like You. ~Prayer song by

1978 Bud John Songs, Inc. (Admin. by EMI Christian Music Publishing)

~~~~~~~~~~~~~~~~~~~~~~~~~~~~~~~~~~

The Diva

This one seems self-explanatory, but maybe does not strike you as being someone who would be in Christian leadership. Ms. Green describes her: "This bridesmaid manages to make your wedding all about her. She insists on planning the shower her way and around her schedule, and on the big day spends more time primping for the camera than you do." While on the surface and even down to the depth this diva bridesmaid should not represent a Christian, much less a leader, we are a fallen people who have to die daily to self-will.

Today's Christianity consists in large part to a pastor-centered church structure. This is due to a couple of things. If the pastor is the center of the workings of the church, then he or she is responsible to get it done. The responsibility of the rest of the congregation is to show up and pay tithe, which is the only thing that a pastor cannot do on his own. This works for a lot of Christians today for various reasons. It also works well for pastors who like to be the one people count on, the one in charge, the one in control. Self-sacrifice is the way they live their lives to the glory of God. The problem is that the sacrifice is on their terms, which is why the word of God reminds us that obedience is better than sacrifice.

I do not want to put too much definition here or give examples, but I want to interject as a staff pastor that this diva mentality can take up residence here as well. I work on a staff of 10 pastors where one of them is our lead pastor and we are all partners together. While our lead pastor has understood (seen in his actions) that the ministry of our local church is not dependent upon him, there have been times that we as staff pastors have battled within ourselves the mentality that the ministry could not operate without us. The ministry that we were in charge of was all about us. Though we are loyal to the vision of the lead pastor, we have this embodiment of our ministry that is self-serving and non-inclusive. So whether it is pastor centered or staff centered, the Big "C" Church should be individuals that make up the Bride of Christ, and they should have as the center of their will and being Christ Himself. The little "c" church, local and beyond should be about building up and equipping the Bride of Christ. We should be about the Father's business, not our own.

There are a few things the rest of this article helps us to diagnose and remedy in the diva leadership mentality. First, talk and spend time with the people you lead. If you hear their heart and you share yours, while prayerfully seeking to do God's will, then the love of Christ will guide you in how to sew the tapestry together in your area of leadership. Second, another help stated in the article is to look back at hurts and losses that may be playing into a fear that you have. I know that when we have to have control of something it is usually because we have fear of what could happen if things get out of control. Prayerfully look back and see if there is any bitterness or hurt, especially in ministry, that is not resolved and reconciled. Third, make sure that you are not comparing yourself to others. This is another trick of the enemy to start you down the path of thinking about yourself. It seems at first that you are just trying to sharpen your skills or learn from one another, and while that is good, keep a close eye on comparison. The best way to do this is to get the right perspective, which leads us back to the most powerful way to avoid being a diva… be a person of prayer. If you are constantly in the Presence of the Living God by turning your eyes on Him, then your heart will be open and yielded to His will.

Scripture Meditation:

John 3:30 – "He must increase in importance, while I must decrease in importance."

Matthew 23:25 – "How horrible it will be for you, experts in Moses' Teachings and Pharisees! You hypocrites! You clean the outside of cups and dishes. But inside they are full of greed and uncontrolled desires."

Lord, help me to give up my right to myself and to give up my plan and purpose and yield to the zeal that you have for your Bride. From the depths of my heart show me the steps to take in order to be about your business with every conversation, ministry decision, staff appointment, and order of service. Be glorified, not just in me Lord, but in your Church so that your church may glorify you. I know that it is all about you Jesus, but by your life and death, you are all about people, so Lord show me your plan and purpose to reconcile all people to yourself and make them into ambassadors and priests as you have purposed to do. In Jesus' Name, Amen.

The Rookie

"This is the first time she's ever been asked to be a bridesmaid. She doesn't know she's expected to help shop for dresses, plan the shower and bachelorette party, and show up at pre-wedding events. You may feel hurt that she's not more involved." Hopefully, if you have been a leader for some time you can look back and remember when this was true for you. I think that it is good to remember that we are always a rookie at something. It is like always having a learner's mentality. If you cannot remember this, then you are a rookie who is new to leadership or you're a leader who has never been told you are a rookie. Sometimes because of position, people tend to overlook the obvious. When you are assigned or you enter a situation where other people are around you but they do not know you, they have expectations, not grace for you, and you have expectations, not grace for them. A lot of bitterness and hurt stems from this rookie ingredient. Whether you are entering a role or entering new territory, being a rookie in leadership is necessary or no one would be in leadership. So since this is part of the overall plan of God to prepare His Church for acts of service, then it seems that we should embrace and not despise it.

The dilemma of this aspect of leadership is that most seasoned leaders do not want to remember or be faced with or have to deal with ignorance and immaturity. Also, rookies do not know they are rookies unless they are told. When they are told, because they are rookies, they seldom believe you. Now if you are laughing right now you have been and have dealt with a few rookies in your time or you are a parent of a teenager. The hard part about coming of age as a seasoned leader is that God will bring more rookies your way because He can trust you with them. I am not sure which aspect to go with here, being the rookie or dealing with rookies, since if you are mentoring rookies for the first time, you are a rookie. Then I think it might be best to stick to the "this is me" revelation of the rookie.

My friend says that she reminds her children regularly as they grow from year to year that she has never been the mother of a 14 year old and a 16 year old. A good reminder for leaders to remember as they lead others, we can all be rookies together. Being a rookie, according to John Wesley, is not a sin because by definition we do not know any better. However it is important, just as a teacher's main goal is not to teach a student the material but rather to teach a student how to learn the material. A better example is that you do not give the hungry fish; you teach them how to fish. So it is with being a rookie, we have to learn how to learn while keeping in mind some of the barriers to learning. I know that seems like I am beating around the bush or just beating the bush itself, but think about it. The definition of a rookie is a probationary beginner or first timer. Probationary means people are watching. This is actually always the case in leadership, but the microscope is on for rookies.

So what is the microscope exactly looking for? In a healthy environment, they are looking for how you react and respond to being a rookie. Abigail suggests a few things that I think are helpful to all sides of the relationships here. "Don't take (the rookie's) inaction personally." That advice is fairly clear for those that are welcoming the rookie; but from being in the rookie mentality, humility is essential, realizing that you may not even be aware that you are not aware. Open communication and feedback is necessary with ears wide open to what those around you might be trying to help you realize. Remember the best, most seasoned leaders will not outright tell you "what's up". They know better. It is best if reality of leadership is revealed to you as time progresses, but be the greenest apple you can be in this situation.

Of course, just because you are new, this is not an excuse to drop responsibilities. The first step is actually recognizing that you are a rookie in the situation, then asking the right questions so that you have a better chance of knowing what most people just assume you know. Small details or routines are not easily transferred to a newbie, but because you are new you will pick up on things just by listening to stories from previous years or circumstances from those who have been there longer than you. So the same advice to the diva comes to the rookie as well… listen… listen to the stories, experiences, even taped sermons, etc. from before you came around. This will be helpful in learning the culture that you are being called to -not just to enter but also to equip. Remember always that you are there not by human decision alone, but primarily because our God has positioned you there. He works through authority. He was not a rookie, but He made Himself a little lower than the angels and put on human form to become just that. He grew in wisdom and stature and in favor with God and man. God knew that being a rookie was part of the human condition, a valuable part, so do not despise your youth or this time of growth. One of my favorite sayings is, "The journey is the destination."

Scripture Meditation:

Philippians 2:6-8 – "Although he was in the form of God and equal with God, he did not take advantage of this equality. Instead, he emptied himself by taking on the form of a servant, by becoming like other humans, by having a human appearance. He humbled himself by becoming obedient to the point of death, death on a cross."

2 Corinthians 5:14-17 – "Clearly, Christ's love guides us. We are convinced of the fact that one man has died for all people. Therefore, all people have died. He died for all people so that those who live should no longer live for themselves but for the man who died and was brought back to life for them. So from now on we don't think of anyone from a human point of view. If we did think of Christ from a human point of view, we don't anymore. Whoever is a believer in Christ is a new creation. The old way of living has disappeared. A new way of living has come into existence."

1 Timothy 4:12 – "Don't let anyone look down on you for being young. Instead, make your speech, behavior, love, faith, and purity an example for other believers."

Lord, I know that You have called me not only to Yourself, but also to shepherd Your sheep. I may be a rookie, but I am filled with Yahweh Tsabaoth, The Lord of Hosts. Father, in humility knowing that it is only because of You that I stand, I do indeed stand in the position and authority that You have placed me. Remind me that I am in Your plan. "In", not a part of, but completely within and under Your wing. "Your", not my "Plan" not job, not responsibility, not expectation. Help me Lord to BE in You as a rookie and beyond. Amen.

~~~~~~~~~~~~~~~~~~~~~~~~~

The Critic

On my first day on staff as a pastor, my senior pastor came in and said to me, "The price of leadership is criticism, lead on." John Maxwell tells of a friend that said to him, "If you are getting kicked in the rear, it means you're out front." While both of these statements are very true and should be taken to heart by anyone in leadership who is being criticized by those you are leading, let's take a different approach here. This critic is one who is critical of those they are leading or responsible for. I know as a leader, I have reached the point where if someone that I am responsible for says something very harsh to me, I may suffer a little, but my skin has thickened and I take it with a grain of salt. However, if I am criticized by someone in authority over me, that is a whole other ballgame. One who is supposed to lead me, equip me, encourage me, teach me has an open line to my loyalty, my submission and my respect. So when criticism travels down that pipeline, things become personal very fast. I respect the authority that God has over me and I trust them to carefully lead me. So when I turn things upside down and zero in on my own style of leadership, am I a critic? Maybe your first response would be no, but especially if you are a type A personality, goal oriented leader you should think through things using a word that may not have such a negative connotation. Critique is from the same root word. This seems positive enough, right?

It is the Holy Spirit who convicts of sin, who reveals error, who guides and directs ultimately. He uses us as His vessels to polish and smooth out the edges as iron sharpens iron. In my experience that has been from a peer or friend, not a leader unless I specifically asked for it or if they did not know that the Holy Spirit was using them to talk to me. For example, I live in the Shenandoah Valley in Virginia. When I moved here I was looking for a church to call home. After going to a few churches, I realized that I had the power to change sermons just by walking in. I knew that I wanted a church where dressing casually was acceptable so I dressed the part. While I did not think that small earrings and makeup would step on toes, I walked into a few churches on

61

Sunday morning and did just that unknowingly. When the pastor began to preach, his sermon changed sometimes to a whole new message and sometimes just enough to make his point. The point was how a woman should dress and what is appropriate and inappropriate. Perhaps I was wrong in my unchanging strategy of finding a church by dressing the part. However, criticism by a leader of the church did not have the sweet aroma of forgiveness that accompanies the conviction of the Holy Spirit. Obviously highlighting a difference of interpretation and opinion is one way where criticism gets out of hand, but also when I apply this to myself. I believe that the most important thing to bring before God is my heart. A leader should not have a critical heart, but one full of grace, mercy and love. The blood of Jesus makes this not only possible, but in light of God's mercy, essential. The goal of making the Bride ready, I believe, rests in the heart of every Christian leader, however, remembering that the end result is not what God is interested in first and foremost. He is not about religion or checking the list of what does not measure up, but rather about the relationship, the love that grows between us as we encourage each other daily. Christ is the tie that binds. He is the love between us as Christians and John tells us that He did not come into the world to condemn the world but that through Him the world might be saved. Nothing has changed. God is not a taskmaster, but rather a loving Father. He bids us to be the same type of leader, loving and full of mercy and grace.

Scripture Meditation:

Colossians 4:6 – "Everything you say should be kind and well thought out so that you know how to answer everyone."
1 Peter 3:15-16 – "But dedicate your lives to Christ as Lord. Always be ready to defend your confidence in God when anyone asks you to

explain it. However, make your defense with gentleness and respect. Keep your conscience clear. Then those who treat the good Christian life you live with contempt will feel ashamed that they have ridiculed you."

Lord, teach me gentleness, I know that You are the one who convicts and makes Your Bride holy not on the outside, but on the inside. Help me know rest in You through prayer and supplication when the hearts of those that You have entrusted me to shepherd seem to be turned away from You. Father, guard my heart so that I may be a stepping stone, not a stumbling block. In Jesus Name, Amen.

~~~~~~~~~~~~~~~~~~~~~~

The Loner

To whom much is given much is required. We hear this, quote this and while it is biblical, let's put it in context. This verse is written in the Gospel of Luke, from the parable of the three servants found in Matthew 24 and 25. Jesus is speaking to the servant who is left in charge, which does speak to us as leaders, but read what Luke 12:47-48 says:

"The servant who knew what his master wanted but didn't get ready to do it will receive a hard beating. But the servant who didn't know what his master wanted and did things for which he deserved punishment will receive a light beating. A lot will be expected from everyone who has been given a lot. More will be demanded from everyone who has been entrusted with a lot."

When we look at ourselves as leaders, there are a few directions that we are likely to go in when we get a glimpse of the big picture of which our Big God has allowed us to be in; not only in the picture but in charge and responsible for a group of His flock. We could put our nose to the grindstone and drive ourselves out in front so far that as we are striving to do what we are called to do, we actually get further and further from the real goal... making disciples. On the other hand we could also get so stressed out from the big picture and the glimpse of God's vision that we begin to think and act like it is ours to accomplish, when in fact the Bible tells us the zeal of the Lord Almighty will accomplish this....through us. This paralysis tends to spread and we end up being ineffective as a leader. We are ahead of the flock, but since the flock is not going anywhere we are really just standing to the side slightly. Another way that we can become the loner is not so much being separated from our local flock by way of too much work or by way of busy work, but rather to blend in so much as a part of the flock that we isolate the flock from the other flocks because we refuse to associate with other shepherds of other flocks.

It is my belief that most of Christendom suffers from extreme loneliness. Since we belong to the family of God and this family is strong when we come together as God has intended, our leaders ought to be cornering the market on this truth, but instead we are leading the pack when it comes to isolation. Paul gives us insight into how we should be in spite of how those we lead are in 2 Corinthians 6:11-12, "We have been very open in speaking to you Corinthians. We have a place for you in our hearts. We haven't cut you off. Your own emotions have cut you off from us." Discipleship making is personal. We are not leading an organization or a model of what church should be, but people who make up the Body of Christ. We are alive and as opposite to reality as it seems, we are to be one.

I am the leader who has forgotten the big picture too often and in one way or another secluded myself all the while believing that I am leading. Some of the things which I do in seclusion are beneficial and necessary in taking care of me as a leader. We need time alone with God, we need time alone with our thoughts, we need time alone with our family, but we cannot abstain from activities that are important in the lives of the people we lead, like baseball games and family fun nights. These are the places where the stories that open people's ears on Sunday morning come from. These activities pave the way for entering not just into the lives of the people but into their community of influence as well. Jesus did this well. He led His disciples by being with them, living with them and entering the lives of their families. He entered Zacchaeus' house, He spent time at the house of Lazarus, Mary and Martha in Bethany. He was involved; He was in the company of those He led. The times in the Gospels where it speaks of Jesus going off by Himself to pray were unique enough to include. He was not a loner.

Scripture Meditation:

John 15:15-17 – "I don't call you servants anymore, because a servant doesn't know what his master is doing. But I have called you friends because I've made known to you everything that I've heard from my Father. You didn't choose me, but I chose you. I have appointed you to go, to produce fruit that will last, and to ask the Father in my name to give you whatever you ask for. Love each other. This is what I'm commanding you to do."

John 17:11b-12 – "Holy Father, keep them safe by the power of your name, the name that you gave me, so that their unity may be like ours. While I was with them, I kept them safe by the power of your name, the name that you gave me. I watched over them, except one person, *who* became lost. So Scripture came true."

Abba Father, thank you that You are not a distant God, but you are Emmanuel, right here, right now with me. Forgive me when I have not followed Your hand of grace into the lives of those You have entrusted me with. Increase my compassion and give me wisdom and depth of insight to know how to reach into their lives in the name of the One called Friend who sticks closer than a brother. In His name Jesus, Amen.

~~~~~~~~~~~~~~~~~~~~~~~~~~~~~~~

The Whiner

Much like the diva, this leader has a bad case of it's all about me, but the key ingredient here is the motive not the outcome. While pride and control motivates the diva, the whiner is motivated by none other than discouragement, lack of courage. No matter where you sit in leadership there are times when your vision grows dim, your faith wavers and you find yourself whining. A leader may not seem whiny, they usually know better than to get in the pulpit and whine or to sit down with one of the flock and whine, but you see it when they sit down with other leaders or with their family. One of the hardest balancing acts in ministry is to figure out how to be with your family. If you are the primary pastor of the church, then most of the time your family either does not have a pastor or does not have a spouse/parent.

Don't take this too critically, if you work in a job that takes you out of the home more than half the week or if you work for your spouse the same is true. It is a hard balance to maintain. One thing that happens is you let the family in on life in ministry or a situation that starts out being just an "in the know" session becomes a venting or whining session.

While I did not grow up in ministry, my stepfather owned a company where a lot of my family members and extended family worked at one time or another. He would come home and share with the family. The only thing from his life that he could share and build family relationships with was company talk, which at times could turn into a grown man with a deep voice whining about how things are going or how people are acting. This was fine and dandy until he touched on a family member or one of their departments, then there was a defense mode and stress levels began to rise. If a solution or answer to his frustration could be reached then we worked it out, but many times there was not a direct answer so he whined. As the whining continued, it became the passive aggressive way to send a signal out to manipulate anything possible within other relationships. This is certainly a recipe for disaster.

While I have been writing this segment, I have been thinking about the conversations that I have with other leaders and explaining how to go from whiner to leader in all situations. Then my husband walks in. He has just taken our little Shih Tzu, Wasabi, out on his daily walk to do his daily business. We live in a resort area where some people have second homes and when they come in, they disrupt our lives. So here is the scenario. Our neighbors, who are very sweet people, come in and bring their dog that loves to roam and does not like to be cooped up. My husband and Sabi come down the driveway and instead of sniffing and being about his business, my dog thinks it's playtime and completely ignores his need to go potty on a very cold morning. My husband comes in the door and began to tell me about the dog and how our dog would not comply or do his business because of this distraction. Before I knew the neighbors or considered them part of our street, I would have been with him in the complaint, but rather I began to think how do I turn this whine to shine? How can this discouragement turn around to build relationship? With courage. It seems so easy to say that my husband should have a conversation about what our routine looks like and what might be a few solutions that both dogs could benefit from. That is the exact same solution for those of us in ministry. "Keep the conversation going" is another piece of advice that helps in this situation to have courage to overcome discouragement.

The key to losing the whine is to know what things to only bring to God in prayer and cast your care, and to know what things you should have a conversation about with those who are the cause of frustration. How do you know? Well you could talk with the people first and see how well that goes, or a better solution is to go to the Lord first and cast all of the cares on Him, and then allow Him to open the doors to have the conversations with those who are involved. One of the best gifts that God gives is the present. Rehashing yesterday or earlier today is not living in the present. Being anxious about later today or tomorrow is not living in the present. Relationships are built on shared experiences, not on sharing experiences. The main thing to remember in the case of the whiner is that as a leader we have a responsibility to lead, not get caught up in the chit chat of things.

Scripture Meditation:

Timothy 2:4 - "Whoever serves in the military doesn't get mixed up in non-military activities. This pleases his commanding officer." 2 Remember where the fight is and we have direct access to the commander-in-chief. When you find yourself whining, stay on your knees till the whine turns to shine.

Philippians 4:6 - "Do not be anxious about anything, but in everything by prayer and petition with thanksgiving present your requests to God. And the peace of God which transcends all understanding will guard your heart and your mind in Christ Jesus."

The Serenity Prayer

God grant me the serenity
To accept the things I cannot change;
Courage to change the things I can;
And wisdom to know the difference.

Living one day at a time;
Enjoying one moment at a time;
Accepting hardships as the pathway to peace;
Taking, as He did, this sinful world
As it is, not as I would have it;
Trusting that He will make all things right
If I surrender to His Will;
That I may be reasonably happy in this life
And supremely happy with Him
Forever in the next.
Amen.
--Reinhold Niebuhr

The Had-To-Ask-Her

In all of my years of being a real bridesmaid, which totaled up to three times, I was always the had-to-ask-her. I was the sister of the groom twice and the cousin you grew up with but did not see much anymore. So I am so familiar with this in reality but in the theory and symbolism of what we are using this for, I had to think how this would apply. After weeks of mulling it over in my mind… (I admit halfheartedly) as I sit here I remember the feelings in both circumstances. The first… I love the groom. I want what is best for the groom, but who is this lady that thinks that she has what it takes to make him happy. The second… I love the bride. I want what is best for the bride, but are we sure that her trust is in the right groom or is she being deceived. Relationships are a funny thing. Let's translate this into ministry. There have been so many times that I have walked with people who have worn out my kid gloves, trampled my long-suffering and yet still claimed to love Jesus. As a bridesmaid, I am called to serve the bride. To treat those who seek Jesus like I would treat Jesus Himself who is always faithful and true. I am to do this without judgment, since He judges the hearts of men. I have to do this with mercy and grace since that is the environment of the New Covenant. Are you getting the mixed emotions that a Had-to-Ask-Her Bridesmaid goes through? While it may seem that this minister is lacking in her love for the bride of Christ, it is more rooted in her trust in the Groom. We must trust His plan, His way, His process, Him.

I was at a camp one summer and while you may not know my pastor, many on our district either knew him at one time or have heard about how the Lord has blessed many through him. One new pastor on the district asked me point blank, "What is it about my pastor as a leader that is so different from other Christian leaders?" I was stunned by the question and more by the answer that flew from my lips before I even had time to really think. "He trusts God with His people." We could say "He trusts the Groom with His Bride." I do not know if you can fully appreciate what I came to re-emphasize over and over. I have never watched someone walk in rest throughout every situation not controlling today but trusting in "the God who holds tomorrow".

So whether you love the groom and are not sure about the bride or you love the bride and are not sure if they completely see the right groom, trust THE GROOM to work all of that out. This is a journey, not a destination, to have relationship with the Groom. While we look forward to the Wedding Supper of the Lamb, we know that the relationship and revelation of the Son through His Body begins now. The Bible even has the reaction of some people who are trying to ascertain the motives of people preaching Jesus. In Philippians 1:18 Paul tells us, "But what does it matter? Nothing matters except that, in one way or another, people are told the message about Christ, whether with honest or dishonest motives, and I'm happy about that. Yes, I will continue to be happy." Being a minister is a privilege and an honor. This is not a requirement of the Christian walk or a relationship with Christ. Once you have put your hand to the plow of serving and loving Jesus, do not look back, but take some advice from my pastor who encourages, especially senior pastors, to take a sabbatical and allow the Groom to renew your love and call. So rejoice in relationship and rejoice in the wedding celebration and trust God with the details.
Scripture Meditation:

1 Timothy 4:12-16 "Let no one look down on your youthfulness, but rather in speech, conduct, love, faith and purity, show yourself an example of those who believe. Until I come, give attention to the public reading of Scripture, to exhortation and teaching. Do not neglect the spiritual gift within you, which was bestowed on you through prophetic utterance with the laying on of hands by the presbytery. Take pains with these things; be absorbed in them, so that your progress will be evident to all. Pay close attention to yourself and to your teaching; persevere in these things, for as you do this you will ensure salvation both for yourself and for those who hear you."

Lord, sometimes I have felt unwanted and unneeded as a leader. Sometimes I did not want to be there or had mixed emotions in doing what You have asked me to do. Help me not to think with my feelings but rather to live as a testimony to You. Lord, may the words of my mouth and the meditations of my heart not only be acceptable to You but also be useful for teaching and building up. May they not fall short in reach because of lack of love or faith. Help me to trust You more with Your people. In Jesus' Name Amen.

~~~~~~~~~~~~~~~~~~~~~~~~

The GEM

Abigail Green describes the Gem as the one "who knows the true meaning of friendship." Jesus says of his disciples that he no longer sees them as servants, but calls them friends. Why, because they love Him; He knows this because they obey Him. Ephesians 4 tells us that we are God's gift to the bride. The verb "to give" means "to bestow without receiving a return; to confer without compensation; to impart, as a possession; to grant, as authority or permission; to yield up or allow." This sounds much like the point of John 15:12-17, "Love each other as I have loved you. This is what I'm commanding you to do. The greatest love you can show is to give your life for your friends. You are my friends if you obey my commandments. I don't call you servants anymore, because a servant doesn't know what his master is doing. But I've called you friends because I've made known to you everything that I've heard from my Father. You didn't choose me, but I chose you. I have appointed you to go, to produce fruit that will last, and to ask the Father in my name to give you whatever you ask for. Love each other. This is what I'm commanding you to do."

For God so loved the world that He gave…

God's favor has been given to each of us. It is measured out to us by Christ who gave it… He gave apostles, prophets, missionaries, as well as pastors and teachers… Ephesians 4.

Christ laid down His life for His friends. We too should not only take up our cross and follow Him, but lay down our lives for Him. We are His to give. He gives us to His body, His bride; and He tells us, whom He has empowered, what our goal is. We are to equip the bride to serve and to build up the body of Christ. This is a big job.

How can I fulfill that purpose? The first step is to stop thinking about the questions with "I" in them so much. If we rephrase the questions, then the answers can be closer to the right perspective. Maybe, how can we fulfill that purpose? If we realize that we are one of many bridesmaids with the same mission and vision, then the perspective widens to encapsulate a better picture of the bride. But I think the best question to ask is "Lord, what next?" I realize that is probably the opposite of thinking big and having a wider perspective. I realize that God gives awesome, amazing vision in order to motivate and encourage the people we lead, but I really believe that the best bridesmaids are the ones who are giving constant attention to the will of the Groom. This is where the analogy stops in light of today's weddings. Basically today the bride calls the shots and what she says goes. It is her day so to speak. But in a perfect world, and I know that brides have voiced this when it is all over, she really did not know what she wanted all along. It would have been better if she would have not had the stress of getting all of it done and only concentrated on her budding relationship and living in the present and presence as the day approaches. To be honest, I do not even know the wants and true desires of my heart from time to time, except to know Christ more.

Scripture Meditation:

Isaiah 6:8 "Then I heard the voice of Adonay, saying, "Whom will I send? Who will go for us?" I said, "Here I am. Send Me!"

Lord, Fill me with your Spirit and empower me to be a bride that lives in the present in constant relationship with my Groom. Have absolute sway over me as a yielded vessel ready to do and be your will. Your Word tells us Your bride has made herself ready. Lord, I give myself anew to You ...use me, impassion and empower me that Your bride may be found faithful and true awaiting the day of Your Glorious Return. Come Quickly, Lord Jesus, Amen.

Chapter Seven

The Heart of the Father

The body of Christ is made up of people from every nation, tribe, and tongue, male and female. The voice of God does not proceed from the lips of one person, but rather a myriad of people, who have experienced life and the Life Giver in different ways. It would be a gross understatement to say that God cannot be fully represented by one culture or type of person. Yet most of my life I have been very partial to a few types of people teaching me and preaching the word of God to me. The heart of God beats in His surrendered people. The heart of the message is preached and taught in His surrendered leaders.

One aspect or perspective that I can offer from my own experience at least will add to the many perspectives through which we can know and experience God. In making this confession of sorts, I believe that if you are open this will help you give grace to pastors who love God and are female.

I have made the statement, and I know that some other leaders have made this statement as well. "Some of our best men are women." While I would have backed it wholeheartedly six months ago, God is helping me. I would say this when questioned about being a female pastor. After sitting in service one Sunday, I heard the statement and it hit me in a different way, kind of like a culture click. Let me write this and let me know how it hits you. "Some of our best white men are black." In our culture today, we understand how wrong this statement is, however, I had not made that leap of understanding for the previous statement yet. When I heard this, God began speaking to me over the next several months gently telling me, "I created you as a woman, if I had wanted you to be a man, I would have made you one, so why don't you stop trying to be a male pastor and start being the pastor I called you to be."

God created me personally to be a woman. I was created to be an image bearer of God. When God created Adam and Eve, God created them to be His image bearers. He created Adam first and then he took a bone from the side of Adam and formed Eve. He did not remove something from Adam like an appendix, but rather the verb for take or remove implies that he took a significant piece from Adam to make Eve. So that in Adam, who was created in the image of God, a load bearing wall was removed. Now Adam and Eve are image bearers of God. Each person who God creates uniquely in their mother's womb bears the image of God. Since we are all different, different characteristics of God are seen in our strengths.

In trying to process my own journey, I was telling a pastor friend of mine that I represent the mother heart of God. He corrected me and gave me his perspective. He helped me to reconcile my wording with my understanding. Here is my response via email... I certainly did need his viewpoint.

"I know that I used the term 'mother heart of God' and after some thought, even though when I first heard that term I understood it one way, with something said yesterday it is not the best terminology for what I mean. I think you said something like not wanting us or

76

anyone to feel impotent or unable to represent God in some way. I think the better way to put it is that the HEART of God is given and fills yielded men and women, since the Spirit of God knows the heart of God and reveals it to us. The terminology 'mother heart of God' is wrong since it really seems to say that God has a mother heart and a father heart that He reveals to woman and man respectively. Since that is nonsense, I want to clarify… We say Father God, but understand that He is not limited or divided by gender or race."

God fills each of us as we yield to Him and sets us apart to do His will and His purpose. Since He created us, He uses our unique styles and gifts to accomplish His will through us. One of the things that make us unique is our gender. So while He does not have a heart divided at all, there are attributes of God that, for instance, a female pastor is better gifted to reflect than a male pastor, partially, not totally because of their gender.

I know this seems nerdy and "science-y", but just like the waves of sunlight enter a prism and because of the intricacies of the prism, that determines what light is seen. (Knowing God can shine through a donkey I understand, but I also realize that He created us in our inmost being to do what He had in mind for us to do from the foundation of the world).

A single parent can serve and must serve both roles in parenting; they must step up and be disciplinarian and nurturer. While both qualities are parent qualities and exist in each parent, it is only when the mother and father are both present that the father is truly free to be a father and the mother is truly free to be a mother. While that looks different in each family, the image bearers of God are able to more fully represent Him when both genders are present, just like the Church more fully represents God when we are together and represent different nations and colors.

I did not answer the call of God right away because I did not believe that I could and because of not wanting to make waves. I have had people get up and walk out when I get up to preach, and while it did not bother me mid-message because the Spirit of God was upon me I have had to find a way to deal with those feelings and struggles afterward. All the while asking God why I should bother preaching and leading in roles that a lot of my brothers and sisters in Christ, at their core, believe is unbiblical. I should just let my brothers answer that call since it is You, God, that is speaking through them and you can use one voice just as you use the next one. After wrestling with these and other questions, as always it simply comes down to obedience. I understand in part, but not fully. In part, God has reminded me that it is not about me. Not at all! Whether male or female, however, His voice is better understood through many unique and creative vessels. Being limited to part of the church limits God. God's response to me personally has been that His children are suffering because the heart of a woman, filled with the words of God and the experiences of a woman enlightened by the Spirit of God, are muted and the Church has a single parent mentality. With that, any mother knows that any opposition or question or hesitation to move forward was overwhelmed by the mother heart that God has given to every woman.

This confession is from my heart. I believe that God has called many leaders for such a time as this. I am sorry if this confession flies in the face of the core of your theology; please forgive what you would consider my ignorance and only hear what God would say to you through this book. However, if you are resisting a call to be a bridesmaid for the Bride of Christ and for whatever reason you feel inferior or unwanted or unappealing or unprepared or even abominable, get over yourself. Concentrate on Him and worship Him in the way that He has gifted you.

Chapter Eight

The Wedding Day

For generations, we have looked and identified this world as hell on earth. We understand that the reality of hell is the absence of the presence of God. So while we live in a very depraved generation, we are the presence of God in this world. We are His Kingdom, if He is our King. All of the problems, sickness, sin, and debauchery that are in the world should remind us that we are in the world, but not of the world. However in our mindset we wonder how Christ, our Bridegroom, can wait to return for His Bride. The world is getting worse and worse and it will not be long for the signs of the times to click forward and, because of how bad things have become, Christ will return. Many of my experiences in church have been dependent on the church gathering, preaching and singing about how we are to endure until this world gets so bad that these signs happen and then the Father will send the Son.

While Matthew 24 talks about the signs of times, I want to look again at Revelation 19:7.

Let us rejoice and be glad

 And give him glory!

For the wedding of the Lamb has come,

And his bride has made herself ready.

The blood of Jesus Christ cleanses us from all sin, the Bride and Bridesmaids have made the Bride ready. The Bride is known and made beautiful to all by the righteous deeds that come not only because she is cleansed, but also from a pure heart. The Bridesmaids, being in the Bride in reality, are also responsible for supporting and encouraging the Bride to spur her onto being ready.

The ultimate call in the Christian walk is not what some would call full time ministry. I believe we have mixed up in some circles the call to being set apart, the call to holiness. We call people to come out from among them and be separate, but we liken that to being an equipper. I am sorry but that is not our call. We cannot call people into ministry. We have two bells, two calls to mankind. I remember an old preacher who used to pastor in New York City, who has since gone on to be with the Lord. Brother Harold Thompson would come up to me and say there are only really three invitations in the Bible. Remember while God initiates all of them, with two of them we welcome people, and one of them we welcome God.

1. "'Come now, and let us reason together,' Says the LORD, 'Though your sins are like scarlet, They shall be as white as snow; Though they are red like crimson, They shall be as wool.'(Isaiah 1:18)

2. "Then Jesus said to His disciples, 'If anyone desires to come after Me, let him deny himself, and take up his cross, and follow Me.'" (Matthew 16:24)

3. And the Spirit and the bride say, "Come!" (Revelation 22:17

The two calls that we have to mankind are the freedom from the penalty of sin and the power of sin, and to salvation and sanctification.

The third call is the essence of what this book is about. Within all of these calls there is not one blanket call that goes out to find leaders, because we do not find or call out leaders; God calls them as He chooses and gives them as gifts to the Body of Christ. So when we call for the next step in Christianity, while leaders may answer His call within the call, we are not calling for them, we are calling for holiness unto the Lord. We are waving the lantern for sinners and for the redeemed. The call is the same, intimacy, but it is two-fold: accept Jesus' life sacrifice and be forgiven, and yield your life as sacrifice and be holy.

When God created the world, His creation did not have any rebellion or push-back, it was good, very good. However, after sin entered the world and self-will no longer chose God and His ways, we went our own way, and this rebellion and push-back broke the heart of our Father. He then sent His Word, His Beloved Son into the world to grow in wisdom and stature to be an example and teach us how to yield and willingly choose the One who created and has loved us from the beginning. He was our example of the way of purity and love. Jesus was recognized publically by the Father at His baptism, His transfiguration, His death, His resurrection and His ascension. The Father was inviting the people to understand that the Son does exactly as the Father wills and that He is the exact representation of God. You know all of this, as a leader and as a Christian, you understand and realize these things, but I want to make the leap from the Bridegroom to the Bride here. When Jesus was on earth, He and He alone was the person that set the Father in motion as He learned obedience and chose to do the will of the Father. What of the Bride, will her ascension be any different?

Thanksgiving is approaching as I am writing this and I have turkey on the brain. People are sharing recipes with me and asking how the turkey is going to be prepared this year. While my dad used to deep fry his turkey and I usually buy one already cooked, when I think about cooking it in the traditional sense I cannot look at the turkey from the outside and tell whether it is done or not. I cannot even cut into the turkey and see if all is done. I could use the meat thermometer, but I would much rather buy the turkeys with the red dots on them. That way I put it in the oven and wait for the red dot to pop out. That is one way to explain what I believe the Father is doing while He is tarrying to sound the call for the return of Christ.

Many times in my Christian walk, I have been waiting on God, only to find out that really the entire time, He was waiting on me. What if the same thing is happening as we await the return of the One called Wonderful. God is waiting for the Church to pop out, to be separate, to come out from among them, to be holy. What if this entire time we have come close to being ready but, because we were looking at the world and how bad it is to gauge our response or looking at end time events that God brings to pass to measure the times, we miss the point. The return of Christ rests in the Bride being ready, this does not depend on the world, and God has done and continues in love and grace to do His part. It is the Church that we are a part of and it is the Church that we are waiting for. Is she ready, has she made herself ready? Is she set apart by a pure heart and righteous deeds, or are we sitting on our laurels and worrying more about this world and its possessions instead of the Kingdom?

There is an Old Testament story in Genesis 19 about Sodom and Gomorrah. This is another example of the righteous being in the world, but not of the world. The angels came to Lot's house because he was righteous and set apart from the godlessness. As the story continues, Lot and his wife and daughters flee to a nearby town as the cities are being destroyed. I have the same picture in my mind as the red dot popping out of the turkey. (Don't judge me☺). The only difference in this instance was that Lot's wife was not completely separate; she still had affection for that world. She died because she was not ready to come out from among them. So this begs the question, now in this age of grace where God has said that He is patient and not willing that any should perish, how many times has the Bride of Christ been almost ready by being set apart with her eyes fixed on Him, then she looked back? The Father had "Go get her" on the tip of His tongue and then He hung His head, because we lost sight of Christ, we got distracted.

Now do not take this to be condemning. I believe that God is revealing exactly what we need when we need it and while His heart longs for us to be with Him, He is working all things together for those that love Him and are called according to His purpose. This world must not be too bad if we still choose it and what it has to offer over Jesus. Oh to be like the song, "Take the whole world, but give me Jesus". So as this world becomes less appealing to us, we "consider it pure joy, my brothers and sisters, whenever you face trials of many kinds, because you know that the testing of your faith produces perseverance.

Let perseverance finish its work so that you may be mature and complete, not lacking anything." (James 1:2-4)

The Holy Spirit is the only one that knows the very heart of the Living God. This same Spirit dwells within us. When I was writing this out, I wrote that the Holy Spirit cries "Come!" and the Bride cries "Come!", but when I looked up the reference for it, I realized a beautiful truth. The Spirit's desire is that of the Father and the Son, to bring us to Himself so that we may be where He is, but it is the other part of the equation that is not complete. Revelation 22:17 reads, "The Spirit and the bride say, 'Come!'" They are one as the cry of their heart rings out. The Bride who is ready and can only think of her Bridegroom.

Going back to what Jesus said in Matthew 24, while He begins talking about the end of the age in answer to a question by His disciples, He ends His lesson with a corporate view of the Church, a corporate view of the Bride who is attended to by wise and faithful servants. We have a lot of work to do, and we must be about His business.

Recently, during the funeral of a prominent member of our community, there were many ears present to hear the saving grace of Jesus Christ. With such an opportunity for open hearts to hear, my pastor was reflecting on the harvest potential. It was then that the Holy Spirit impressed his heart with this question, "Are you ready?"

The leader of the largest Sunday School Ministry in the world, Bill Wilson once said, "Tragedy does not change people, the Presence of God changes people." So, are we ready?

In order to minister in the name of Jesus to a broken world, His presence, His Spirit needs absolute sway in us as leaders and in His

Church, His ambassadors. Knowing God's prevenient grace is always at work wooing people to Himself, may our hearts be one with His Spirit, then we will be able to unite with the Spirit of the Living God in Revelation 22, "Come, Lord Jesus!"

www.ingramcontent.com/pod-product-compliance
Lightning Source LLC
Chambersburg PA
CBHW071833020426
42331CB00007B/1713

* 9 7 8 0 6 1 5 6 4 7 5 1 7 *